Captain Maxi's Secret Island

By V. Gilbert Beers

Illustrated by Helen Endres

MOODY PRESS • CHICAGO

What You Will Find in This Book

© 1983 by V. Gilbert Beers
Library of Congress Cataloging in Publication Data

Beers, V. Gilbert (Victor Gilbert), 1928-
  Captain Maxi's secret island.

  (The Muffin family picture Bible)
  Summary: Thirteen Bible stories paired with
stories of the Muffin family, in which the lesson of
the Bible story is applied to everyday life.
  1. Bible stories, English. [1. Bible stories.
2. Christian life–Fiction] I. Endres, Helen,
ill. II. Title. III. Series: Beers, V. Gilbert
(Victor Gilbert), 1928-　　. Muffin family
picture Bible.
BS 551.2.B429 1983   220.9'505   82-14540
Printed in the United States of America

TO PARENTS AND TEACHERS

CAPTAIN MAXI'S SECRET ISLAND is a book about Bible people… and a family like yours. Half of the stories are Bible stories, about God at work in the lives of Bible people. With each Bible story is a matching Muffin Family story, applying the truth of the Bible story to everyday life. The Muffin Family is a family like yours and mine. They are not sugarcoated, but make the same mistakes and do the same wrong things that we do. But they solve their problems as a Christian family should, with the help of God and His Word. At the close of each Bible story, the principal Bible truth is clearly stated. Several questions help you and your child think about that Bible truth. At the close of each Muffin Family story the application of that same Bible truth in family life is clearly stated. Several questions help you and your child apply that truth in your own lives. The Muffin Family members are role models, showing principles of Christian living in action, in the lives of true-to-life people. Application is one step closer to reality in your family. This volume is the eleventh in a series called *THE MUFFIN FAMILY PICTURE BIBLE*. These volumes put Bible and life application side by side, truth and fantasy side by side, and bring these all together at one certain place. In this volume, it is Captain Maxi's Secret Island. Previous volumes in the series are: *THROUGH GOLDEN WINDOWS, UNDER THE TAGALONG TREE, WITH SAILS TO THE WIND, OVER BUTTONWOOD BRIDGE, FROM CASTLES IN THE CLOUDS, WITH MAXI AND MINI IN MUFFKINLAND, OUT OF THE TREASURE CHEST, ALONG THIMBLELANE TRAILS, TREEHOUSE TALES,* and *MUFFKINS ON PARADE.*

TROUBLE IN THE FAMILY

Family Jealousy

Genesis 29:31–30:43

Jacob never wanted four wives! He dreamed of marrying one lovely girl. One day he left home in Beersheba and went far to the north to find her. There he met Rachel and fell in love with her.

"I'll work for you seven years if you let me marry her," Jacob told Laban, Rachel's father.

Laban's eyes sparkled. Seven years of free work from a strong young man. What a good deal that was for him!

"Yes!" said Laban.

At the end of the seven years, Laban gave a big wedding party. Late at night, when it was dark, Laban brought Jacob's bride to him. Jacob thought it was Rachel. But when morning came, he found that Laban had brought Rachel's older sister Leah instead.

"You tricked me!" Jacob shouted angrily at Laban. "I want to marry Rachel."

"You will marry her," said Laban. "But since Leah is the older sister she has to get married first. It's the way we do things here."

Jacob felt trapped. He didn't want two wives. He was in love with Rachel. He wanted to marry her. But he had been forced to marry Leah first.

"Promise that you will work for me another seven years," Laban told Jacob. "I will let you marry Rachel next week."

Jacob promised, and he married his true love, Rachel. But did they live happily ever after? No, because Jacob had two wives. They grew jealous, even though they were sisters.

The jealousy became worse when Leah had a son. It's always an honor to have a baby. But in those days it was a special honor to have a son. Rachel was jealous because she had no children yet. Then Leah had another son, and another, and still another.

By this time Rachel was worried. She still had no children. What could she do? Then she thought of a way. Her people at that time thought this way was right. We know, of course, that it isn't right.

"Take my servant girl Bilhah and live with her as your wife," Rachel told Jacob. Rachel would think of Bilhah's children as her children.

Now Jacob had three wives. The three were in a race to see who could have the most children. Bilhah soon had two sons, so that was two for Rachel's side. Leah already had four sons, so she was ahead. But she had not had a child lately.

Leah was afraid now that Rachel and her maid Bilhah might catch up to her. So she decided to do what Rachel had done.

"Take my servant girl Zilpah and live with her as your wife," Leah told Jacob. Leah would think of Zilpah's children as her children.

Now Jacob had four wives. Rachel and her maid Bilhah wanted to have the most children. But so did Leah and her maid Zilpah. No wonder there was so much jealousy in the family!

Time passed. At last Jacob had eleven sons and one daughter. He had a big family to feed and take care of. But Jacob was still working for Laban. He was not getting paid for his work. Laban instead gave Jacob and his family what they needed. But Jacob wanted to earn his own money.

"It's time to go home to Beersheba," Jacob told Laban one day. "Let me take my family and go."

But Laban did not want to let Jacob go. Jacob had worked hard for him. Laban was much richer now.

"I'll pay you!" Laban offered.

"Don't give me money," Jacob answered. "Just give me your sheep and goats with streaks and spots."

Laban smiled. That was a good deal for him. There weren't many animals like that.

It was also a good way to tell which animals belonged to Laban and which belonged to Jacob. All the plain colored sheep and goats belonged to Laban. All the streaked and spotted animals belonged to Jacob.

But as time passed more and more streaked and spotted animals were born. Soon there were more of those than the plain colored animals. Jacob was getting richer while Laban was getting poorer.

Now some other family members grew jealous. Laban's sons did not like this and complained to Laban. They thought Jacob was cheating Laban.

By this time Jacob was surrounded by jealous family members. Jacob must have wondered if things would ever work out right for him.

If only Jacob could have looked ahead. If only he could have seen what God would do through his family. But he couldn't. Instead, he saw his family torn apart by jealousy.

WHAT DO YOU THINK?

What this story teaches: A family can be torn apart by jealousy. This happens when family members want to get more than they give.

1. Why were Jacob's wives jealous? How did they try to get rather than give?

2. Why were Laban and his sons jealous? How did they try to get rather than give?

3. How do you think Jacob felt about his family at this time? How do you think the Lord felt about it?

Sailing on the Golden Tub

A Muffin Make-believe Story

It was only an old washtub. The mast was a broomstick with a sheet for a sail. But to Captain Maxi and his crew it was much more. No pirate ship was faster, or more beautiful. No ship could sail the seas better than the Golden Tub.

That's what happens when you use a little imagination!

The wind caught the sails, and the Golden Tub was off to adventure. Nobody knew where. Nobody cared.

"Sails aloft, First Mate Mini!" Captain Maxi bellowed. "Batten down the hatches, Navigator Tuff! Stow the cargo, Boatswain Ruff!"

First Mate Mini wondered how you batten down hatches. But she thought it best not to ask.

"Raise the boom!" Captain Maxi bellowed. "Right to starboard, you swabs!"

Captain Maxi kept on bellowing. The first mate ran to do this. The navigator ran to do that. And the boatswain ran in circles, barking.

"My turn!" First Mate Mini said when they were far out to sea.

"Your turn to do what?" asked the captain.

But First Mate Mini didn't answer. Instead, she began to bellow orders. "Mop the swatches!" she shouted. "Stow the cannons in the galley!"

Captain Maxi stood with his mouth wide open. "That doesn't make sense," he complained.

"Neither did *your* orders!" the first mate snapped back.

"Mutiny!" shouted the captain. "You're jealous because I'm captain."

The first mate knew that was true. She wanted to be captain of the Golden Tub. She *was* jealous!

"And you're jealous, too!" First Mate Mini shouted at the captain. "You want to be captain. But you're afraid I'm going to take over. Right?"

The captain knew that was right. Suddenly he was jealous. He liked being captain. He didn't want First Mate Mini to take over.

While the captain and the first mate argued, Navigator Tuff began to meow and "pffft." She wanted to be captain, too! Of course Boatswain Ruff wasn't going to be left out, so he stood at the edge, barking as hard as he could.

"See what you started?" Captain Maxi snapped at First Mate Mini. "We have four captains. But no one is sailing this ship!"

That was true. While the four captains were shouting and barking and meowing and "pfffffting," the Golden Tub was sailing on its own. But it was sailing straight for a strange island.

"Look out!" First Mate Mini shouted. But it was too late. The Golden Tub ran aground. The four fearless sailors were stuck on a strange island.

"See what happens when we have four captains?" asked Captain Maxi.

First Mate Mini hung her head. "You're right!" she said. "No ship can have four captains. No ship can have even two captains. To show you how sorry I am, we'll name this island 'Captain Maxi's Secret Island.'" The navigator meowed happily, and the boatswain barked his friendliest bark. Then the four went off the Golden Tub to explore Captain Maxi's Secret Island.

LET'S TALK ABOUT THIS

What this story teaches: Families, and ships, can be torn apart by jealousy. We are happier, and God is happier, when we help one another.

1. Why was First Mate Mini jealous? How did this make Captain Maxi jealous?

2. Why can't a ship have four captains? What will happen?

3. Are you ever jealous? Are you ever jealous of your brother or sister? What does the Lord think about that?

4. What happened to the Golden Tub? What can happen to your home if you stay jealous? What should you ask the Lord to do when you get jealous?

A Family That Could Not Stay Together
Genesis 31

Everyone wants a happy family. Jacob did too. But things didn't work that way.

Jacob wanted to marry Rachel. He and Rachel would have their own home. They would have children. And they would live happily ever after.

But trouble started when Rachel's father tricked Jacob. He made Jacob marry Rachel's older sister Leah first. Jacob didn't want to marry Leah. He didn't want a second wife. But he had to do it to marry Rachel.

The two wives were sisters. But they were jealous. Their jealousy led them into a silly contest to see who could have more children.

When people get into a silly contest they sometimes do silly things. Rachel gave her servant girl to Jacob as a wife. Then Leah gave her servant girl to Jacob as a wife. Poor Jacob! He was caught between Rachel and her servant girl and Leah and her servant girl.

Rachel's father, Laban, made Jacob miserable. He made him work for many years without paying him. When Jacob said he would leave, Laban gave him the sheep and goats with streaks and spots. The Lord must have felt sorry for Jacob. Soon most of the animals were born with streaks and spots. At last Jacob grew richer. Laban grew poorer.

Laban's sons were angry and jealous when they saw this. So was Laban.

Jacob knew that he and Laban's family could never be happy living together. One day he took his family and headed home to Beersheba.

Laban and his sons were away. They did not learn that Jacob had left until three days later. When they did find out, they were angry. They hurried after Jacob to make him come back.

The night before Laban found Jacob, the Lord spoke to Laban in a dream. "Be careful what you say to Jacob!" the Lord warned.

When Laban met Jacob the next day he was careful what he said. He did not try to make Jacob come back.

But Jacob was angry about how mean Laban had been to him. He told Laban how he had cheated him.

It was clear to Jacob and Laban that they could never live together happily. Laban must go home. He would never see his daughters or his grandchildren again. Jacob must go back to Beersheba. Rachel and Leah would never see their father again. They would never see their brothers again. And their children would never see Grandfather Laban again.

The Lord must have been very sad to see this family who could not stay together. The Lord wants to see families live together happily.

Jacob and his relatives piled many stones together. These stones would separate Jacob and Laban for the rest of their lives.

"I will never go past this pile of stones to hurt you," Laban told Jacob. "And you will never go past this pile of stones to hurt me." As far as we know, Laban and Jacob never went past the pile of stones again, even for a friendly visit.

Everyone must have cried as they parted. It's sad to see a family that cannot stay together.

WHAT DO YOU THINK?
What this story teaches: Everyone is sad when a family or friends cannot stay together.
1. What happened to this family to tear them apart? Why could they not stay together?
2. What would you have said to Laban to help the family stay together? What would you have said to others in the family?
3. What did the Lord probably think about all this?

Pippin's Place

A Muffin Make-believe Story

"Let's explore!" said Captain Maxi.

This time First Mate Mini did not argue. She did not try to give orders. And she was not jealous.

Captain Maxi, First Mate Mini, Navigator Tuff, and Boatswain Ruff set out to see Captain Maxi's Secret Island.

They had not gone far when they saw a charming little cottage. Four little pippins were still building it.

"Oh, look!" said Mini. "Isn't that darling!"

"Looks good enough to eat," said Maxi. "But isn't that different? One side is made of lollipops. Another is made of peppermint. Another is gingerbread, and the other is made of gumdrops."

"And there's one little pippin working on each side," said Mini. "Let's go talk to them."

"I'm Peppermint Pippin," said the pippin working on the peppermint side. "He's Lollipop Pippin." He pointed to the pippin on the lollipop side. "Let me guess," said Mini. "That must be Gingerbread Pippin working on the gingerbread side."

"And Gumdrop Pippin working on the gumdrop side," Maxi added.

"Verrrrry good!" said Peppermint Pippin. "But you came at a bad time. We pippins are having an argument."

"That's terrible," said Maxi. "Mini and I never argue." Mini giggled. She remembered the big argument they had about being captain of the Golden Tub.

"Well, we don't argue much," Maxi said. "But why are you arguing?"

"We're building Pippin's Place," said Peppermint Pippin. "But it must be built of peppermint. It's the only way to do it."

"He's wrong!" Lollipop Pippin interrupted. "As you can easily see, lollipops are the best building materials."

"Gumdrops!" shouted Gumdrop Pippin.

"Gingerbread!" shouted you-know-who.

"Peppermint!"

"Lollipops!"

"Gumdrops!"

"Gingerbread!"

"Oh, my," said Mini. "Now they are really arguing. I'm afraid we only made their argument worse."

The four pippins argued long and loud. They said some things that even pippins should not say.

At last Peppermint Pippin threw down his peppermint blocks. "I can't work with you other pippins!" he shouted. Then he walked away.

"I can't work with you pippins, either!" shouted Lollipop Pippin. Then he threw down his lollipops and walked away.

"I can't work with you pippins, either!" shouted Gingerbread Pippin. He threw down his gingerbread boards and walked away.

"I can't work all alone!" shouted Gumdrop Pippin. He threw down his gumdrop bricks and walked away.

"They're gone!" said Maxi.

"Now Pippin's Place will not be built!" said Mini.

"All because of an argument," said Maxi.

"I'm glad WE never argue," Mini said with a giggle.

LET'S TALK ABOUT THIS

What this story teaches: It's sad when families or friends can't stay together or work together.

1. Why did the pippins argue? What caused each to go his own way?

2. Do you know anyone who argues with others in his family? Do you? What will you ask the Lord to help you do?

3. Do you know of a family that could not stay together? Why do you think this happened? How can the Lord help families that are about to separate?

A Family That Came Together Again

Genesis 32-33

Jacob was so happy to see Laban go back home. Laban was his uncle, his mother's brother. He was also the father of Jacob's wives, Rachel and Leah.

But Laban had not been a good uncle or father-in-law to Jacob. He had cheated Jacob and made him work for nothing.

Jacob should have felt free. He should have felt good about going home to Canaan. But Jacob was worried.

Twenty years earlier Jacob had run away from home. He had left because his brother Esau wanted to kill him. Jacob had tricked his father into giving him something Esau wanted. That made Esau very angry.

Now that Laban was gone, Jacob began to wonder about Esau. Did he still hate Jacob? Did he still want to kill him? Would he? There was no way for Jacob to know the answer to those questions. That's what made him worry.

Jacob knew he couldn't keep on worrying. He had to find the answer. So Jacob sent some messengers to see Esau.

But Esau would not tell the messengers if he hated Jacob. He would not tell them if he would kill Jacob. Instead, he told them that he would come to see Jacob–with four hundred men!

When Jacob heard this, he worried even more. He felt almost sure now that Esau would kill him. Perhaps he would kill all of Jacob's family too.

Jacob did not have enough men to fight Esau. What could he do? First he divided his family into two parts. *If Esau kills one part, perhaps the other can escape,* Jacob thought.

Then Jacob did what we should do at a time like that. He prayed. He told the Lord how good He had been to Jacob. Then he asked the Lord to protect him from Esau.

Next Jacob prepared some expensive gifts of animals for Esau. He sent one servant toward Esau with goats. He sent another with sheep. He sent another with camels. Another went with cows and bulls. And another went with donkeys.

The servants were spaced so that Esau would meet one every few minutes. Each servant would say, "These animals are a gift from Jacob."

When Jacob was alone that night, the Lord came to him. The Lord looked like a man.

The Lord wrestled with Jacob all that night. When morning came, the Lord gave Jacob a new name.

"From now on, you will be called 'Israel,'" the Lord told him.

Before long Esau rode up with his four hundred men. Jacob must have trembled, waiting to see what Esau would do. He was almost sure Esau would kill him and his family.

Instead, Esau ran up to Jacob and hugged him and kissed him. Jacob had worried about something that didn't happen.

For twenty years Jacob and Esau had been a family divided. But with that one hug and kiss, Esau brought his family together again. It was now a family that had found forgiveness.

WHAT DO YOU THINK?
What this story teaches: Forgiveness can bring a family or friends together again.
1. Why did Jacob worry so much about Esau? What did he think Esau would do?
2. What really happened when Esau and Jacob met? Do you think Jacob was surprised?
3. When family or friends are divided, what will bring them back together again?

Riding from Painted Pony Stables

A Muffin Make-believe Story

"Where did the pippins go?" asked Mini.

"One went north. Another went south. One went east. Another went west," said Maxi.

"Oh, dear, how can we ever get them together again?" asked Mini.

"We'll never do it walking," said Maxi. "We need horses or cars or something. I wonder what they have on this island?"

Maxi didn't have long to wonder. Maxi, Mini, Ruff, and Tuff soon came to a clearing among the trees. They saw a charming little building.

"Painted Pony Stables," Mini read. "Oh, Maxi. Look! Just what we need. Ponies!"

"Painted Ponies!" said Maxi. "I hope we can ride them."

"You can ride them if you pretend you can ride them," said the stable boy. "But that shouldn't be hard, since you're pretending all this anyway."

23

Before long, Maxi and Mini were riding awa
their painted ponies. Ruff rode with Maxi.
rode with Mini. Away they went across Ca[
Maxi's Secret Island.

"I never knew painted ponies could ride like t
said Mini.

"They can't," said Maxi. "But since this is a
tend island, we can pretend anything. Can't v

"Oh, yes," said Mini. "And what fun to ride
way. Just wait until I tell my friends back hon

"But we have more important work to do n
said Maxi. "We're off to find the pippins. Firs
head north to find Peppermint Pippin."

The painted ponies seemed to know where t
Soon they found Peppermint Pippin, sitting
log. He looked so sad.

"Your friends will forgive you if you come
to Pippin's Place," Maxi shouted.

Before Peppermint Pippin could say a word, N
and Mini were riding to the south. The painted pc
seemed to know where to go. Before long they f
Lollipop Pippin, sitting on a log. He looked so s

"Your friends will forgive you if you come ba
Pippin's Place," Mini shouted.

Before Lollipop Pippin could say a word, Max
Mini were riding to the east. The painted pc
seemed to know where to go. At last they fc
Gingerbread Pippin, sitting on a log. He looked so

"Your friends will forgive you if you come ba
Pippin's Place," Maxi shouted.

Before Gingerbread Pippin could say a word, .
and Mini were riding to the west. The painted p
seemed to know where to go. It wasn't long b
they found Gumdrop Pippin, sitting on a lo;
looked so sad.

"Your friends will forgive you if you come back to Pippin's Place," Mini shouted.

Before Gumdrop Pippin could say a word, Maxi and Mini were riding back to Pippin's Place. When they got there, what do you think they saw? Four pippins were standing with their arms around each other. Each had asked the others to forgive him. Each looked happy now.

Of course, it didn't take long for them to build Pippin's Place. Now they were all working together.

LET'S TALK ABOUT THIS

What this story teaches: Forgiveness can bring a family, or friends, together again.

1. Why do you think each pippin was sad? What did Maxi and Mini say to each one? What made them happy?

2. When we say things, or do things, that need to be forgiven, are we happy or sad? What should we do to be happy again?

3. Look up Ephesians 4:32 in your Bible. What does it say about forgiving?

4. Is there someone you should forgive? Is there someone who should forgive you? What will you do now?

GOLDEN CHEST

When the Ark Was Captured
1 Samuel 4-5

"Take the Ark of the Covenant from the Tabernacle?" Eli repeated. "Take it to the battlefield? Oh, no! Never! It has always been here in the Tabernacle. God told Moses to put it there almost four hundred years ago."

Old Eli, high priest of Israel, was right. This beautiful golden chest was made by Moses and his men. God had told them how to make it. He had given Moses the Ten Commandments on tablets of stone. Moses had put them in this beautiful chest.

But now the leaders of Israel wanted to take the Ark from the Tabernacle. They wanted to take it to the battlefield.

The Israelites and the Philistines were fighting at that time. But the Israelites were losing. Thousands of them had been killed. Now the leaders thought the Ark might help them win the battle.

"But we must take it to the battlefield," they told Eli.

Old Eli was ninety-eight and blind. By this time his two sons Hophni and Phinehas decided what would happen there at the Tabernacle. So after Eli sputtered and grumbled a few times, Hophni and Phinehas took the golden chest from the Tabernacle. They carried it to the battlefield.

When the soldiers of Israel saw the golden chest they shouted as loud as they could. They shouted so much that it seemed that the earth shook.

These men thought the Ark had some special power. They thought this power would help them win the battle.

But they were wrong. They expected too much from the Ark. God had the power to help them win the battle. The Ark did not. The men should have trusted in God to help them. But they didn't. They trusted in the golden chest, the Ark. And they lost the battle. Thousands of them were killed. Hophni and Phinehas were killed too.

The battle was lost. The Ark was captured. Quickly a messenger ran with the news. Eli sat near the Tabernacle, waiting to hear what was happening.

"Israel has lost!" the messenger told Eli. "Your two sons are dead. The Ark has been captured."

It was too much bad news. Poor Eli fell over and broke his neck and died.

The Philistines hurried back home with the Ark. They too thought the Ark had some special power. They thought they could keep this power from the people of Israel. If they could, they would keep the people of Israel from winning any battles.

The Philistines put the Ark in the temple of their god, Dagon. Dagon would watch over it. He would keep it safe. But the next morning Dagon's statue was lying on the floor.

The Philistines set the statue up again. But the next morning it was knocked down again. This time it was broken. Then the Philistines became very sick.

Now the Philistines began to learn something the Israelites should have learned. It wasn't the chest that had the power. God had the power! He was more powerful than their god, Dagon. He was more powerful than their people. He was more powerful than all their cities. And God did not want the Philistines to have His golden chest.

"Send it back to the Israelites!" the Philistine people told their leaders. So the leaders made plans to send it back.

WHAT DO YOU THINK?
What this story teaches: Boxes or buildings or things do not have power to do God's work. Only God can do that!
1. Who made the Ark? What was in it?
2. Why did the Israelites want it on the battlefield? What did they think the Ark would do for them? Did it?
3. Could the Ark help them win the battle? Who could do that?

30

Old Wells and Water Buckets
A Muffin Make-believe Story

"I'm thirsty," Mini complained. "Where can we find water on Captain Maxi's Secret Island?"

"We'll have to explore," said Captain Maxi. "It's a good thing we can ride the painted ponies while we are on the island."

The painted ponies seemed to know the way. Before long Maxi and Mini, Ruff and Tuff rode up to an old well.

"Oh, Maxi, isn't that DAR-ling," said Mini.

Maxi and Mini stood for quite a long time, looking at the beautiful well. They were sure they had never seen such a nice well before.

"I'm thirsty," Mini said at last.

"Looking at the old well won't take away your thirst," said Maxi. "Only the water inside will do that."

"Then we must find a bucket to let down into the well," said Mini.

It didn't take long to find the bucket. It was hanging on the end of a rope. The rope was tied to a handle.

"Oh, Maxi, look at the beautiful old wooden bucket," said Mini.

It was a beautiful old bucket. Maxi and Mini stood for quite a long time, looking at it. They were sure they had never seen such a beautiful old wooden bucket before.

"I'm thirsty," Mini said at last.

"Looking at the old wooden bucket won't take away your thirst," said Maxi. "Only the water inside the well will do that."

"Then we must crank the bucket down into the well," said Mini.

It was such fun to crank the bucket down into the well. When it hit the water it made a big splash. Maxi and Mini did it at least ten times. Each time they let the bucket down, Mini squealed. What fun!

"I'm thirsty," Mini said at last.

"Cranking this old bucket down won't take away your thirst," said Maxi. "Only the water inside the well will do that."

"Then we must bring some water up in the bucket," said Mini.

Maxi and Mini cranked the bucket up to the top. The water in the bucket looked cool. It swirled around and around in the bucket. Maxi and Mini watched the water swirling and splashing in the bucket.

"I'm thirsty," Mini said at last.

"Watching this water swirl and splash in the old wooden bucket won't take away your thirst," said Maxi. "Only the water in the bucket will do that."

Mini dipped some water from the bucket with a cup. She put the cup to her mouth. Then she drank all of the water in the cup.

"Now I'm NOT thirsty," Mini said at last.

"The water did that!" said Maxi. "Looking at the well couldn't take away your thirst. Looking at the bucket couldn't take away your thirst. Cranking the bucket up and down couldn't take away your thirst. Even looking at the water couldn't take away your thirst. But *drinking* the water *could!*"

Then everyone else had some water – Maxi, Ruff, Tuff, and even the painted ponies.

LET'S TALK ABOUT THIS

What this story teaches: Wells, buckets, or cranks will not take away your thirst. Only water will do that. Boxes, buildings, or things will not do God's work. Only God can do that!

1. Why couldn't the well or the bucket or the crank take away Mini's thirst? What could? What did?

2. How do wells and buckets and cranks remind you of the Bible story? The golden chest called the Ark couldn't do God's work for Him. Who is the only One who can do God's work?

3. When you're thirsty, what do you want? When you need help, whom do you want?

The Ark Comes Home
1 Samuel 6:1–7:1

"Send it back to Israel!" the Philistine people shouted.

It was about time! This beautiful golden chest had brought nothing but trouble to the Philistines.

Months before the Philistines and Israelites were fighting. The Israelites were afraid when the Philistines began to win.

"Bring the Ark to the battlefield," the soldiers of Israel cried out. They thought this beautiful golden chest would help them win. They should have known that only God could do that.

The Philistines were excited when they captured the Ark. They thought this golden chest was like a magic charm. They thought that somehow God's power was in the chest.

But God showed them how wrong they were. When the Philistines put the Ark in the temple of their god Dagon, He knocked down Dagon's statue. The Philistines set the statue up. But God knocked it down again. That time He broke it.

In Ashdod, the city where the Philistines put the Ark, the people began to get sick. Rats ran through the streets. They took the sickness to others. Before long people all over Ashdod had big lumps called tumors.

34

"Send the golden chest away!" the people of Ashdod begged.

So the Philistines took the Ark to Gath, another of their cities. But as soon as the Ark came to Gath, the people of that city became sick. Rats ran through the streets of Gath. They took the sickness to others. Before long people all over Gath had big lumps called tumors.

"Send it away!" the people of Gath cried out.

The Philistines took the Ark to Ekron, another of their cities. But the people of Ekron became sick. Rats ran through their streets. They took the sickness to others. Before long people all over Ekron had big lumps called tumors.

"Send it away!" the people of Ekron cried out.

"Send it back to Israel!" the Philistine people cried out.

"How?" the Philistine leaders wondered. Then they asked their priests.

"Put it in a new cart," the priests answered. "Make little golden rats and little golden tumors. Put these in the cart. This will show that we are sorry."

The Philistine leaders did as their priests said. Then they hitched two cows to the cart. These two cows had young calves. Usually cows with young calves will not leave them. Nothing could pull them away.

35

"If the cows leave their calves and pull the Ark back to Israel, we will know that God has made us sick because we took the golden chest," the Philistines said.

The cows started pulling. They wanted to stay home with their calves. They mooed as if to say "I want to stay home." But they kept on pulling the cart with the Ark back to Israel.

How happy the people of Israel were to see the Ark coming home! They put it in the house of a man named Abinadab. Then they gave his son the job of taking care of the Ark.

The Ark stayed in Abinadab's house for the next twenty years.

WHAT DO YOU THINK?
What this story teaches: Don't want things you shouldn't have. Don't keep things God wants others to have.
1. What happened to the Philistine cities that tried to keep the Ark? Who caused these things to happen?
2. Why did the Lord do these things? Where was the Ark supposed to be?
3. Why did the Philistines send the Ark back to Israel? How did they know the Lord had caused the sickness?

Your Pony, My Pony

A Muffin Make-believe Story

"I want your painted pony!"

Maxi looked surprised. Did Mini really say that? "But...but you already have a painted pony," he said to Mini.

"I want yours!" Mini answered.

Maxi looked even more surprised. Mini HAD said that. She really did want his painted pony.

"But what's wrong with yours?" Maxi asked.

"Nothing! I just want yours," said Mini.

Maxi shook his head. "I don't get it!" he said. "You have a painted pony. I have a painted pony. Nothing is wrong with yours. But you want mine. Why?"

"Because...that's why."

"That's not a good reason, Mini."

"It is for me."

"That's because you're Mini."

"And that's why you should give me your painted pony. You should want to please your poor little sister."

Maxi shook his head again. "Sorry, kid. You've got to give me a better reason than that."

"Because...because I like gold better than blue," Mini answered angrily. "And because I think your pony is better than my pony."

Before Maxi could say anything more, Mini climbed onto his painted pony and began to ride along the beach.

"Coming with me?" Mini called back to Maxi. "You can ride my painted pony."

Maxi stared at Mini with his mouth wide open. He could hardly believe that Mini had done this.

"Give me back my painted pony!" Maxi shouted. But Mini kept on riding as though she had not heard Maxi.

"Be careful!" Maxi called to Mini. "That pony likes to stop too fast. He will throw you off if you're not careful. Be CAREFUL!"

But Mini kept on riding. This time she really didn't hear Maxi. Anyway, it was too late. The painted pony stopped fast, and Mini went sailing over its head.

"SPLASH!" Mini landed in the water. She wasn't hurt, but she was very wet and messy looking.

"I'm sorry I tried to take your pony," Mini said meekly. "I'm sorry I tried to keep it."

Maxi helped Mini climb out of the water. Then he helped her get on her blue pony.

"This is fun!" Mini shouted. "I'm glad we each have the right pony. And I really do like blue."

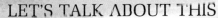

LET'S TALK ABOUT THIS

What this story teaches: Don't want what belongs to others. Don't try to keep what belongs to others, or it may hurt you. God is pleased when we are satisfied with what we have.

1. Why did Mini want to keep what didn't belong to her?

2. Did she try to keep it? What happened to her then?

3. Do you think Mini and Maxi were happier when each had the right pony?

4. Are you happier when you don't want what others have? Are you happier when you keep your own things and not the things that belong to others?

5. Read Exodus 20:17 in your Bible. What does it say? What does it mean? How was Mini coveting Maxi's pony?

Moving God's Way

2 Samuel 6

"Let's bring the Ark to Jerusalem!" King David said.

When a king says something, his people hurry to do it. But bringing the Ark to Jerusalem wasn't as easy as it might seem.

The Ark was a beautiful golden chest. Moses and his friends had made it many years before. God had told them how to do it. They had put the stones with the Ten Commandments in it.

Moses and his people carried the Ark through the wilderness. They brought it all the way from Mount Sinai. They put it in the Tabernacle in the Promised Land.

Now King David wanted the Ark in Jerusalem, the city where he ruled over Israel.

But David forgot to look in the Bible. He forgot to have his people see how God wanted the Ark moved. He forgot to move the Ark God's way.

The day came to move the Ark. The people put it on a new cart. Musicians played. People danced. It was a time to celebrate.

But something happened along the way. A man reached out to touch the Ark. As soon as he did, he fell down and died. Nobody today knows exactly what happened. But we do know that the way he touched the Ark was not God's way.

Suddenly the music stopped. The people stopped marching. Everyone was quiet. Now what should they do?

King David knew then that they were not moving the Ark God's way. "Go home!" the king told his people. He would wait now until he knew what God's way was.

After three months had gone by, King David decided to try again. He must have had some people find out how to do it. They must have looked in the Bible to find God's way. This time men carried the Ark.

The people marched and sang. The king wore a special kind of clothing called an ephod. Trumpets tooted.

Through the gates of Jerusalem they marched. What a time of joy it was! Special times are happy times when we do things God's way, aren't they?

WHAT DO YOU THINK?
What this story teaches: There is a right way and a wrong way to do things. We do things best when we do them God's way.
1. What was the Ark? Why do you think King David wanted it in Jerusalem?
2. What happened the first time David tried to move the Ark? Why did he stop?
3. Why did they move it without any trouble the second time?
4. How can people find out what God's way is? How can you find God's way?

The Painted Ponies' Pony Cart
A Muffin Make-believe Story

"Maxi! Maxi! The pippins are ready to move into Pippin's Place," Mini shouted. "They want us to help them move."

"But we need a cart or something," said Maxi. "Where will we find a cart on this island?"

"Let's go back to Painted Pony Stables," said Mini. "Perhaps they have a cart there."

The painted ponies were happy to take Maxi and Mini back to Painted Pony Stables. They were happy to see the stable boy again. Of course he was happy to see them again too.

"A pony cart? Wait until you see the pony cart we have," the stable boy told Maxi and Mini. "Of course you can use it to help the pippins move."

The stable boy opened a door on the side of the stables. There was the prettiest little pony cart Maxi and Mini had ever seen. It was painted in rainbow colors to match the painted ponies.

"Here's the stuff you'll need to hitch the painted ponies to the cart," said the stable boy. "Sorry I can't help you. I have some chores that I must do. Have fun."

Maxi and Mini thought they would have fun. They thought it would be easy to hitch two little painted ponies to a little pony cart.

But how do you do it?

"These jiggers go here!" Mini argued.

"No, they go there!" Maxi argued back.

So they settled the argument by putting one here and one there. Of course, that is NOT the way to hitch ponies to a pony cart.

To make matters worse, Maxi and Mini got tangled up in the leather straps that were supposed to hitch the cart. There were buckles and straps and gizzmols, and each had a right place. But who knew what that right place was?

"This goes here and snaps to this," Mini argued.

"This goes there and snaps to that," Maxi argued back.

Maxi snapped this while Mini buckled that. By the time they were through the painted ponies couldn't move. Neither could the cart.

"Oh, dear," Mini sighed. "What will we do?"

"Perhaps I can help," the stable boy said. "There is a right way to do this. When you do it the right way, things will work. But when you do things the wrong way, they won't work."

Maxi and Mini did not need to be told that. They could see that they had done things the wrong way. They could see also that their wrong way would not work. They could never move the pippins if they couldn't get the cart to move. They could never get the cart to move if they didn't hitch up the painted ponies the right way.

It looked so easy when the stable boy did it. He snapped this thing to that thing and buckled that thing to this thing. In a few minutes the painted ponies were hitched and ready to go.

"Thank you! Thank you!" said Mini.

"Now we can move the pippins," said Maxi.

LET'S TALK ABOUT THIS

What this story teaches: There is a right way and a wrong way to do things. We do best when we do things the right way. God's way is always the right way.

1. Did Maxi and Mini hitch the pony cart the right way or the wrong way? Did it work? Why not?

2. Which way did the stable boy hitch it – the right way or the wrong way? Did it work? Why?

3. When you do something God's way, is it the right way or the wrong way? Will it work? Why?

MONEY PROBLEMS IN JESUS' TIME

What Not to Do in God's House
John 2:13-25

What would you think if you saw a cow in church next Sunday morning? What if there were cows, sheep, and birds?

Wouldn't you be angry if you saw little booths all over the church? In one booth, a man is selling his cows. In another, a man is selling sheep. And in another, men are selling birds.

Each man is shouting louder than the others, trying to get you to buy his cow, sheep, or birds.

That's what Jesus found when He went to the Temple one day. No wonder He was angry!

The Temple was God's house. It was not made like your church. It had a small building in the center. But the people did not go inside this building to worship. This small building was in an open space called a courtyard, with a wall around it. Outside this wall was a much bigger courtyard. It had a stone floor. But it did not have a roof. There was another wall around that big courtyard.

Jesus saw the men in this bigger courtyard. They had little booths set up. Some sold cows. Others sold sheep. Others sold birds. People bought these animals and birds. They took them to the priests. The priests burned them on an altar.

Doing that was a way to show the Lord they wanted to be forgiven. It was called making an offering.

Jesus was not angry because people bought the animals and birds. He was not angry that they gave them to the priests for an offering. But He was angry that the greedy people bought and sold these things in God's house.

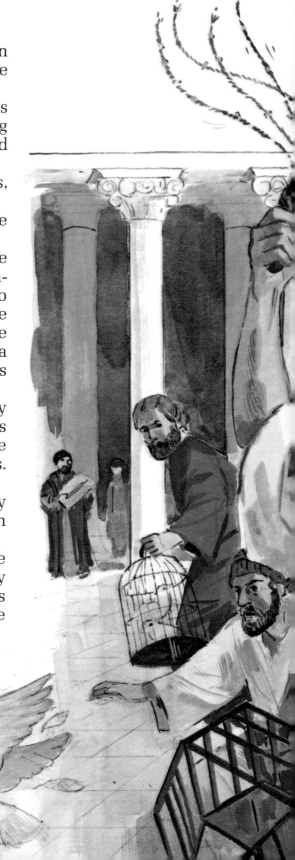

Jesus made a whip. He wove some cords together. Then He went to each booth. He made each man take his animals and birds out of God's house.

"Take these things out of here!" He demanded. "How dare you make God's house a market!"

The men quickly gathered their animals and birds. They picked up the coins Jesus had spilled on the stones. Then they hurried out of God's house. They were afraid of Jesus.

49

Some other men standing there were angry. They told Jesus that they didn't like what He had done.

"Who do you think you are?" they asked.

Jesus tried to tell them. He said that He would rise from the dead someday. But they did not understand what He was saying.

But everyone there *did* understand one thing: There are some things we just don't do in God's house – like buying and selling.

We go to God's house to pray and talk to Him. We go to read His Word and to be with His people. That's why we call it "God's house."

WHAT DO YOU THINK?
What this story teaches: God's house is a place where we can be with God and His people. It is not a market.
1. What were the men selling in God's house? Why did this make Jesus angry?
2. What did Jesus do to these men? What did He say to them?
3. What should we do in God's house? What should we not do?

Sugar Stealer

A Muffin Make-believe Story

"There's Pippin's Place," said Mini.

"And there are the four pippins," said Maxi. "They're waiting for us."

Maxi and Mini rode up to Pippin's Place in the painted pony cart pulled by the painted ponies. They almost looked like a rainbow moving through the woods.

"We're here to help you move into Pippin's Place," said Maxi. "Are you ready?"

"We're ready, but we can't go," said Peppermint Pippin. "If we leave to get our things, there won't be a Pippin's Place when we get back."

Maxi and Mini looked surprised. "Why not?" Mini asked.

"Because Sugar Stealer will eat our house," said Lollipop Pippin. He pointed to a stump not far away. There was a hungry looking fellow, licking his lips.

"Oh, dear!" said Mini. "What can we do?"

Peppermint Pippin sat down by the peppermint side of Pippin's Place to think.

Gumdrop Pippin sat down by the gumdrop side of Pippin's Place to think.

Lollipop Pippin sat down by the lollipop side of Pippin's Place to think.

Gingerbread Pippin sat down by the gingerbread side of Pippin's Place to think.

Maxi and Mini sat down by the painted pony cart to think.

Suddenly Peppermint Pippin jumped up. "I have it!" he shouted. "We'll haul Sugar Stealer to the dump."

Lollipop Pippin jumped up next. "That's it!" he shouted. "Sugar Stealer can eat until he is full."

Gumdrop Pippin jumped up too. "Great idea!" he shouted. "Sugar Stealer will eat so much that he won't want to eat Pippin's Place."

Gingerbread Pippin jumped up last. "Why didn't I think of that?" he said. "Now we can move into Pippin's Place."

"Wait, wait, wait," said Maxi. "Why would Sugar Stealer eat so much at the dump? What would he eat?"

"All the peppermint scraps, lollipop scraps, gumdrop scraps, and gingerbread scraps," said Peppermint Pippin.

"These are the scraps left over when we built Pippin's Place," said Lollipop Pippin.

"We threw them into a big pile in the woods," said Gumdrop Pippin.

"Now Sugar Stealer can have all he wants to eat, and we can live in Pippin's Place. That's why we built it, you know," said Gingerbread Pippin.

53

The four pippins lifted Sugar Stealer from the stump and plopped him into the painted pony cart. Then Maxi and Mini hauled him to the dump.

You have never seen such a happy sugar stealer in your life. There were piles and piles of peppermint scraps, lollipop scraps, gumdrop scraps, and gingerbread scraps.

"Good-bye, Sugar Stealer!" Maxi and Mini called as they drove off with the four pippins.

But Sugar Stealer was too busy eating. He would not stop long enough to say good-bye.

"Now we will move you pippins into Pippin's Place," said Maxi.

"Good!" said Peppermint Pippin. "Pippin's Place will be used the way we builders planned."

LET'S TALK ABOUT THIS
What this story teaches: Things should be used the way the builders planned.
1. When the pippins built Pippin's Place, how did they plan for it to be used?
2. How did Sugar Stealer almost stop the pippins from using Pippin's Place that way? How did Maxi and Mini and the pippins solve that problem?
3. How is Sugar Stealer like the men selling in God's house in the Bible story?
4. How was God's house supposed to be used? How were people using it? What did Jesus do about that?

Jesus Paid Taxes Too!
Matthew 17:24-27

Did you know that Jesus paid taxes? People in Jesus' time had to pay many kinds of taxes, just as we do today.

One tax was called the Temple tax. It wasn't much. Some say it was only about thirty-two cents. But a man had to work two days in the fields to earn that much.

Some men who did not like Jesus tried to trick Him. They tried to make Him say something wrong.

"Doesn't Jesus pay the Temple tax?" these men asked Peter.

Peter wasn't sure. So he said yes. That seemed to be a good thing to say when he wasn't sure. It was better than saying no.

As soon as the man left, Peter rushed into the house to talk to Jesus. He wanted to know if he had said the right thing.

Before Peter could say a word Jesus spoke. He knew exactly what Peter was thinking. He would answer Peter's question before Peter could ask it.

"From whom do kings collect taxes?" Jesus asked Peter. "Do they take this money from their own sons, or do they take it from others?"

"From others," said Peter.

Then Peter understood. The Temple was God's house. Jesus was God's son. Jesus should not have to pay taxes to take care of God's house. Others should do that.

"We don't want to offend these people," Jesus said. "So I will pay My taxes."

Peter knew that Jesus did not have money to pay His taxes. Peter did not have the money to pay *his* taxes, either.

"Go down to the lake," Jesus told Peter. "Throw in your fishing line. When you catch a fish you will find a coin in its mouth. It will be exactly what you need to pay your tax and mine."

Peter must have felt excited as he went down to the edge of the Sea of Galilee with his fishing line. He knew exactly what would happen. When Jesus said something would happen, it always happened that way.

Can you imagine fishing that way? Wouldn't you have fun?

WHAT DO YOU THINK?

What this story teaches: Jesus paid taxes and obeyed the law. It's a good idea for everyone, isn't it?

1. What was the Temple tax? How was it used?
2. Why did Jesus say He should not have to pay it?
3. Why do you think Jesus paid it? If Jesus kept the law, don't you think the rest of us should keep it too?

Pippin Rules

A Muffin Make-believe Story

"Oh, Maxi, look!"

Maxi looked. He had never seen a castle like that before. It was made of peppermint, lollipops, gum-drops, and gingerbread.

"Is this where you live now?" Maxi asked the four pippins.

"Yes, it is," said Gingerbread Pippin. "We'll be so glad to move to our nice little cottage."

"But why?" asked Mini. "This is DAR-ling."

"To you," said Peppermint Pippin. "But have you ever lived in a castle?"

"It's not cozy, like Pippin's Place," said Lollipop Pippin. "It's not as much fun to live in."

"We're so glad we can move to a new little house," said Gumdrop Pippin. "We're glad you will help us move."

Maxi and Mini were sure they would never move from such a charming castle to a little cottage. But they understood what the pippins were saying. A cozy cottage might make a better home.

"You must remember three rules when you help us move," said Peppermint Pippin.

"Never pick up anything by yourself," said Gumdrop Pippin. "You must always have a pippin touch it when you do."

"Never walk through a door first when you are carrying pippin things," said Lollipop Pippin. "You must always let a pippin go through the door first."

"And never set your side down first," said Ginger-bread Pippin. "You must always let a pippin set his side down first."

"Buy why?" asked Mini.

"Who knows why?" said Peppermint Pippin.

"Rules are rules," said Lollipop Pippin.

"They have always been pippin rules," said Gumdrop Pippin.

"So don't ask why, just follow the rules," said Gingerbread Pippin.

60

Maxi and Mini tried to follow the rules. But Maxi grew tired of touching things only when pippins were touching them, walking through doors only when pippins walked through first, and waiting until a pippin set his side of furniture down first.

"These are silly rules!" Maxi said to himself. So when Peppermint Pippin was about to pick up a peppermint statue of some pippin ancestor, Maxi reached out and touched the statue first. The statue crumbled into a hundred pieces.

Maxi was surprised. But he was sure that he had not caused this. So he went to help Lollipop Pippin move a beautiful lollipop-shaped mirror. Maxi grabbed the other side and started to move through the door first. Suddenly the lollipop-shaped mirror cracked into a hundred pieces.

Maxi was surprised. But he was sure that he had not caused this. So he went to help Gumdrop Pippin carry a big chest filled with his favorite gumdrops. When they set the chest down, Maxi put his side down first. The chest broke open, and a hundred favorite gumdrops spilled over the floor.

Just then the four pippins surrounded Maxi, holding hands to make a chain around him. "Rules are rules!" said Gingerbread Pippin. "You MUST follow them if you help us move."

Maxi looked at the hundred gumdrops. He looked at the hundred pieces of the lollipop-shaped mirror. He looked at the hundred pieces of the peppermint statue. He was surprised. But he was sure now that he did cause this.

"I'm sorry!" he said. "I really am. I WILL follow your pippin rules, even though I don't understand them."

"Yes you WILL!" said Mini. Then Maxi and Mini went back to work to help the pippins move. And Maxi followed every rule.

LET'S TALK ABOUT THIS
What this story teaches: Follow the rules! Jesus wants you to do that.
1. What were the three pippin rules? What happened when Maxi did not follow them?
2. What are some rules YOU should follow? What happens when you refuse to follow them?
3. Read John 14:15. What did Jesus say about obeying God's rules? Read Ephesians 6:1. What does this say about obeying your parents' rules? Will you?

Two Ways to Pay a Debt
Matthew 18:21-35

"How many times should I forgive another person?" Peter asked Jesus. "Should I forgive as many as seven times?"

"You should forgive seventy times seven times!" Jesus answered. That was Jesus' way of saying "never stop forgiving."

Then Jesus told a story about forgiving. This is the story.

Once upon a time a king wanted his servants to pay him what they owed him. One important servant had borrowed a large amount of money. It was more than a million dollars.

Of course this servant could not pay his debt. In those days a man who could not pay his debts was in great trouble. This king could sell the man's wife and children and throw the man in prison. That's the way the law was at that time.

And that is exactly what the king said he would do. But this servant fell down on his knees before the king. He was frightened.

"Please, please, please," he begged. "Don't do this. Give me some more time to get the money. I will pay it all back."

The king felt sorry for the man. He didn't really want to sell the man's wife and children.

"Oh, all right," said the king. "I will even forgive your debt. You do not have to pay back the money."

The servant could hardly believe his ears. The king had given him all that money. He didn't have to pay back the million dollars. He got up and ran outside. He was free! He still had his wife and children. And he had all that money.

Suddenly this rich servant saw a much poorer servant. This poor fellow owed the rich servant about sixteen dollars.

"I want my sixteen dollars!" said the rich servant. He grabbed the poor servant and began to choke him.

This poor servant didn't have the sixteen dollars. He fell down on his knees before the rich servant.

"Please, please, please," he begged. "Give me some more time to get the money. I will pay it all back."

But the rich servant would not do this. Instead, he had the poor servant thrown into prison.

Some others had been watching this. They were angry. They told the king what had happened. The king was angry too. He made that rich servant come and bow down before him.

"You are a bad, bad man," the king said to the rich servant. "I forgave you. I forgave your million-dollar debt. Why didn't you forgive the other poor man? Why didn't you forgive his sixteen-dollar debt?"

Then the king had that bad man thrown into prison. He would not get out until he had paid back the million dollars. That meant he would never get out!

"You must forgive others," Jesus told Peter when He finished the story.

Peter found the answer to his question, didn't he?

WHAT DO YOU THINK?
What this story teaches: We must keep on forgiving others.
1. What did the king plan to do at first when the man could not pay back the million dollars? Why did he change his mind and forgive the man?
2. What did the rich servant do to the poor servant?
3. What did you learn about forgiveness from this story? How many times do you want God to forgive you? How many times should you forgive others?

Forgive Me - 302 Times!

A Muffin Make-believe Story

Maxi Muffin stared at the hundred pieces of the peppermint statue. He stared at the hundred pieces of the lollipop-shaped mirror. He stared at the hundred gumdrops scattered on the floor.

"I'm so sorry I caused all this trouble," Maxi said. "Please forgive me."

"I forgive you," Mini answered.

Maxi looked surprised. "I was asking the pippins to forgive me," he said. "I wasn't asking you."

"Don't you want me to forgive you?" Mini asked.

"For what?" Maxi asked, looking surprised.

"For breaking those things and spilling those gumdrops," said Mini.

"But...but those things belong to the pippins," said Maxi. "That's why I asked them to forgive me."

"Do people forgive only if their *things* get hurt?" Mini asked.

Maxi looked confused. "I...I..." he started to say. But he didn't know what to say.

"What about *people* who get hurt?" Mini asked. "Aren't they more important than *things* that get hurt?"

"I...I guess so," said Maxi. "But what does that have to do with you? *You* didn't get hurt."

"Yes, I did."

"How?"

"I have to help you pick up the gumdrops and fix the broken things. So I'm hurt, too."

"Oh!"

"Now do you see?"

"Yes, I guess so."

While Maxi and Mini were talking back and forth the pippins looked even more confused than Maxi. First they looked at Maxi. Then they looked at Mini. Then at Maxi. Then at Mini.

"OK, then," said Maxi. "I'm asking the pippins to forgive me for hurting their things. I'm asking you to forgive me for hurting you and causing you extra work. How's that?"

"That's fine," said Mini. "But how many times do you want me to forgive you?"

"How many?" Maxi looked puzzled. "How many times should you forgive me?"

"Once for the whole thing," said Mini. "And once for each piece I pick up or put together."

"Wow! That's a lot of forgiving!" said Maxi. "There are a hundred gumdrops to pick up. There are a hundred peppermint pieces and a hundred lollipop pieces to put together."

"So I have to forgive you 302 times," said Mini.

"I counted 301," Maxi argued. "Where did you get the extra one?"

"Oh, I just threw in one more in case we missed something," said Mini. "Is that OK?"

"OK," said Maxi. "Now let's get to work and fix those things."

LET'S TALK ABOUT THIS

What this story teaches: Keep on forgiving. It is better to forgive one time more than we should rather than one time less than we should.

1. In the Bible story, how many times did Jesus say we should forgive?

2. What was Mini saying about forgiving when *people* hurt as well as when *things* are hurt? How many times did Mini want to forgive Maxi?

3. Have you stopped forgiving someone for something? Should you? Will you keep on forgiving "one more time"?

A Poor Man Who Became Rich

Luke 16:19-31

Once there was a rich man and a poor man. The rich man had the finest house in town. He dressed in beautiful clothes and ate the richest food.

But the poor man, whose name was Lazarus, had nothing. He was so poor that he often came to the rich man's house to beg for scraps that fell from his table. His finest clothes were rags. Because he had no money for medicine, the sores on his body would not heal. No one gave him ointment or bandages. No one helped him except the stray dogs that licked his sores.

One day the poor man, Lazarus, died. Since he loved God, the angels carried him to the happy place where Abraham was.

The rich man also died. Since he did not love God, he went into hell. There he did not have rich food or clothing or a fine home.

Somehow God let the rich man see Lazarus and Abraham safe and far away. The rich man saw how happy they were. Of course, he knew already how terrible it was to live in hell.

"Father Abraham!" the rich man cried out. "Please send Lazarus. Let him dip his finger in some water and cool my tongue, for this fire is hurting me."

"I can't!" Abraham told him. "There is a great canyon between us. People here can't go there to help you. People in hell can't come here."

Abraham also reminded the rich man of how he had lived on earth. "You had good things there," he said. "But Lazarus did not." The rich man remembered how he had everything and Lazarus had nothing. He remembered Lazarus lying there, begging for his scraps. Now he was sorry. If only he could go back. He would gladly invite Lazarus to eat with him. He would gladly listen to Lazarus tell about God.

Then the rich man remembered his family. Someone must warn them about hell! "Send Lazarus!" the rich man begged Abraham. "Send him back to my father's house to warn my five brothers! I don't want them to come here!"

"The Bible tells them about God," Abraham told the rich man. "Can't they listen to what it says?"

"They will listen if someone comes back from the dead to tell them," the rich man said.

"No, they won't!" said Abraham. "They should listen more to the Bible than to a person who comes back from the dead."

The Bible story ends here. Nothing more is said. It is a sad story about a man who had everything but God. But it is a happy story about a man who had nothing but God.

The rich man was really poor, for all his money could not keep him out of hell. The poor man was really rich, for God took him into His home to live forever.

WHAT DO YOU THINK?
What this story teaches: Listen to the Bible! It tells you how to get to heaven, just as a road map tells you how to get where you want to go.
1. Who had more things on earth, the rich man or Lazarus? Then why did Lazarus go to be with Abraham, while the rich man did not?
2. What did the rich man ask Abraham to do? Why didn't Abraham do these two things?
3. What did Abraham say about people listening to the Bible?
4. Do you read the Bible each day? Do you listen to what God says in it?

Follow the Map!

A Muffin Make-believe Story

"Let's move it!" said Maxi. The pippin things were fixed up and picked up and packed up and tucked into the pony cart. It was time to move the pippins into Pippin's Place.

"We'll go ahead," said Peppermint Pippin. "You come with the cart. Here's a map I've drawn. Follow the map!"

Peppermint Pippin gave Maxi the map, and off went the four pippins. Maxi watched as they headed south on the road.

"Something is wrong here," said Maxi as he looked at the map. "The map says we should go north to get to Pippin's Place, but the pippins went south to get there."

"Follow the map!" Mini said. "That's what Peppermint Pippin told you."

Maxi grumbled a little as he climbed into the cart and headed the painted ponies north. He grumbled some more as they trotted along, pulling the painted pony cart with all the pippin things inside.

"This is wrong!" said Maxi. "I think we should follow the pippins." Maxi stopped the pony cart.

"Maxi! CAPTAIN Maxi!" said Mini. "Follow the map! How can you be a good captain if you can't learn to follow a map!"

Mini had a good point. She hadn't called Maxi CAPTAIN Maxi since they landed on the island. Maxi decided that he wanted to be a good captain on Captain Maxi's Secret Island so he really should follow the map.

That is, Maxi thought this until he got up the road a little farther. Then he began to grumble again.

"It isn't right!" he complained. "They went south. They know the way. We should follow them. This map must be wrong." Maxi stopped the pony cart again.

"CAPTAIN MAXI!" Mini shouted. This time she was almost unMuffinlike in the way she said it. "Peppermint Pippin told you to follow the map. If you want to be a good captain, you must learn to follow orders before you can learn to give orders."

Mini had a good point. Maxi decided that he wanted to be a good captain on Captain Maxi's Secret Island. So he really should learn to follow orders. Then he would know how to give orders.

Maxi began to grumble some more as they came to a curve in the road. He almost stopped the pony cart again. But suddenly Mini shouted.

"There it is!" she said.

Sure enough! There was Pippin's Place up ahead, exactly where the map said it should be. There also were the pippins, smiling and waiting for their things.

"But...but how can this be?" Maxi asked. "Pippin's Place was north on the map. But you went south."

"That's because we're pippins," said Lollipop Pippin. "Pippins go south to get north. It's a good thing you didn't try to follow us. You people must go north to get north."

"Follow the map!" Mini giggled.

"Just like Poppi says about the Bible," Maxi added. "That's God's map. We must follow His map if we want to follow Him."

"Let's move our things into Pippin's Place," said Gingerbread Pippin. So they did.

LET'S TALK ABOUT THIS
What this story teaches: Follow the map! Follow the Bible! You may think you know a better way, but you don't.
1. What would have happened if Maxi had followed the pippins? What did happen when he followed the map?
2. What happens if you follow your own way instead of the Bible, God's way? Why is it better to follow God's way, the Bible?

A Rich Man Who Became Poor

Matthew 19:16-30

"What must I do to live forever?" a young man asked Jesus one day.

"Do you do what the Ten Commandments say?" Jesus answered. Then Jesus reminded the young man what some of the Ten Commandments said: "Don't murder; don't pretend someone's husband or wife is yours; don't steal; don't lie; and honor your father and mother."

Jesus also reminded the young man of another important commandment, "Love your neighbor as yourself."

"I have tried to do these things," the young man said. "Is there anything else I should do?"

Jesus looked at the young man. He was a fine person. He had tried to live a good, clean life. But the young man had thought that this good, clean life would get him into heaven. That is, he thought it until he met Jesus. Now he wondered if there wasn't something else. So he asked Jesus about it.

The young man did not know yet that we get to heaven through Jesus. He did not know that Jesus could forgive sins and give us a new life in Him.

People who have this new life in Jesus want to please Him. They want to do what Jesus wants. They will give up anything if Jesus asks them.

"Will you give up all your money to follow Me?" Jesus asked the young man.

The young man felt sad. He was a rich young man. He had all that he needed. He had all that he wanted. Would he give it up to follow Jesus?

People do not get to heaven by giving up money. People get to heaven by trusting Jesus. He forgives our sins and gives us a new life when we do. Sometimes He may ask us to give up something to follow Him. When He does, we must do it. Sometimes He may ask us to keep our money or things and use them for Him. We must be willing to do that, too.

The young man would not give up his money to follow Jesus. It was too much. He wanted his money more than Jesus. He should have wanted Jesus more than his money.

The young man walked sadly away. Jesus was sad, too, as He watched him go.

"It is so hard for a rich man to go into the kingdom of heaven," Jesus said to His disciples. "It is easier for a camel to go through the eye of a needle."

The disciples were surprised to hear this. How could a camel go through the eye of a needle?

Jesus may have been talking about the eye of a sewing needle. At that time sewing needles looked about the same as they do today. But He may have been talking about the small door that was left open when the city gate was closed at night. It was hard for a camel to squeeze through this little gate. The camel had to be unloaded. Then it had to crawl through on its knees.

"When people give up everything to follow You, what do they get?" the disciples asked.

"They will live forever," Jesus said. "And they will get a hundred times as much out of life."

That's true! To live for Jesus is a hundred times better than to live without Him!

WHAT DO YOU THINK?

What this story teaches: True riches are found in giving, not getting. Our greatest riches are found in giving up ourselves and what we have to follow Jesus.

1. What did the young man ask Jesus? What did Jesus tell him?

2. Why did the young man sadly leave? Why was Jesus sad to see him go?

3. How can you be richer by giving up? What must you do to get to heaven? Do you want to ask Jesus to be your Savior?

A Jar of Wheat or a Truckload of Bread

A Muffin Make-believe Story

"I'm hungry, Maxi," said Mini. "Let's eat!"

"I'm hungry, too," said Maxi. "But what do we have?"

Maxi and Mini had not thought about eating since they landed on Captain Maxi's Secret Island. They had been too busy doing things.

"Let's ask the pippins," said Mini. "They will help us get something to eat."

Peppermint Pippin looked puzzled. "Oh dear," he said. "I don't think we have any people food."

"Pippins eat pippinella," said Gingerbread Pippin. "But you shouldn't eat that! You might get sick or something."

"What about all that gingerbread, peppermint, lollipop, and gumdrop stuff?" Mini argued. "People eat those things."

Lollipop Pippin looked sad. "You WOULDN'T eat our cottage or castle!" he said. "Sorry, but you can't do that."

Maxi and Mini thought about the dump with its leftover gingerbread, peppermint, lollipops, and gumdrops. But they decided it would be no fun eating the dump. Anyway, Sugar Stealer was eating that, and he might get nasty if they came there to eat.

"I...I guess we'll have to stay hungry," Mini whimpered. "And I really *am* hungry."

"Wait!" said Gumdrop Pippin. "I think I have something for you. It's some strange stuff called 'wheat.' Pippins never eat it, but I've heard that people do."

Gumdrop Pippin showed Maxi and Mini a little jar of wheat.

"We could grind it up and make a little loaf of bread," said Mini. "That would give us each a little, and some for Ruff and Tuff, too. But what do we eat tomorrow?"

"Why don't you plant this stuff," said Peppermint Pippin. "It grows in one night. By tomorrow you will have many jars of wheat."

Maxi and Mini looked at each other. They were hungry NOW. But if they gave up the jar of wheat today they would have many jars of wheat tomorrow.

"I say let's eat it now!" said Mini. "I'm hungry."

"Ruff!" said you-know-who.

"Meow!" said Tuff. They were hungry now, too.

"I'm the Captain!" said Maxi. "Right?"

"Right!" said Mini.

"Then I say we plant the wheat so we can have many jars!" So that is what they did.

Mini looked sad as they put the wheat in the ground. Ruff and Tuff looked sad, too. Even Maxi looked sad.

"But we must give it up to get what we need," said Maxi.

Mini knew that Captain Maxi was right and that he had done the right thing. So did Ruff and Tuff.

When the moon came up over Captain Maxi's Secret Island the pippins saw Maxi and Mini, Ruff and Tuff sitting on a little hill, watching the place where they planted the wheat.

"Watched plants won't grow on this island," said Peppermint Pippin. "Better go to sleep."

So with a big yawn, Captain Maxi and his crew lay down and went to sleep.

Imagine their surprise the next morning. When the sun peeked at them they opened their eyes. Guess what they saw? There were beautiful wheat plants with hundreds of grains of ripe wheat on them.

"Enough for a truckload of bread!" said Maxi.

"I'm glad we gave up our wheat," said Mini. "That will give us food to eat as long as we're on Captain Maxi's Secret Island."

LET'S TALK ABOUT THIS
What this story teaches: Sometimes you must give up something before you get what you need.
1. If Maxi and Mini had made bread from the little jar of wheat, would they have had all the bread they needed?
2. What did they do with the little jar of wheat?
3. How did this help them get all they needed?
4. Would you give up something you want to get something you need? Would you give up something you want if it would please Jesus?

TWO MEN OF JERICHO

Bartimaeus-Blind Man of Jericho
Mark 10:46-52

"Help me!"

Blind Bartimaeus had heard the good news. Jesus was coming along the road. He could not see Him. He could only hear the crowd that followed Jesus on the road from Jericho.

"Help me!" blind Bartimaeus cried out to Jesus. "Have mercy on me!"

"Hush!" some people said. "Jesus will not stop to help a blind beggar like you."

But blind Bartimaeus kept on crying to Jesus for help. He knew that there was no one else to help him. There were only a few doctors at that time. They had no medicine that could heal him. And they did not know how to heal a blind man.

"Have mercy on me!" Bartimaeus called to Jesus again.

Jesus stopped. He had heard Bartimaeus. The crowd stopped, too. The people waited to see what Jesus would do.

"Come here to Me!" Jesus called to Bartimaeus. "Jesus is calling for you," some people said. "Get up! Hurry!"

Blind Bartimaeus did not wait to hear more. He threw off his cloak. He groped his way toward Jesus, with some people helping him.

"What do you want Me to do for you?" Jesus asked Bartimaeus.

Of course, Jesus knew. But He wanted blind Bartimaeus to tell Him.

"I want to see," blind Bartimaeus begged. He had never wanted anything more than that.

"You *will* see," Jesus told him. "You will see when you believe."

As soon as Jesus said that, Bartimaeus could see. He had believed that Jesus could heal him and let him see. As he believed that, he was healed.

Jesus went on along the road that led from Jericho. The crowd went with him. But the happiest person in that crowd was Bartimaeus. People could not call him blind Bartimaeus anymore, for he could see the trees and birds and flowers. He could see the crowd. Most important of all, he could see Jesus. That was important, for Bartimaeus wanted to follow Jesus wherever He went.

WHAT DO YOU THINK?
What this story teaches: Jesus will give you what you need as you believe in Him.
1. What was wrong with Bartimaeus? Why didn't he go to a hospital to get well?
2. Why did Bartimaeus call to Jesus? What did he want Jesus to do for him?
3. What did Jesus do for Bartimaeus? What did Bartimaeus have to do to get healed?

Rainbow Paint

A Muffin Make-believe Story

"Would you like to help us paint today?" Ginger-bread Pippin asked Maxi and Mini.

"That sounds like fun," said Maxi. "But what are we painting?"

"Rainbows after the rain this morning," said Peppermint Pippin. "On this island we paint our own rainbows."

"With special rainbow paint," said Gumdrop Pippin. "It's very valuable paint, more precious than gold."

"Wow!" said Mini. "I'm almost scared to use it."

"Pick up a paint bucket at the stable and meet us at the Rainbow Paint Pool," said Lollipop Pippin. "Here's the map! We must go ahead to get things ready."

"Remember, Captain Maxi, follow the map!" Mini said as they went toward the stable in the pony cart.

"I will! I will!" said Maxi. "I learned my lesson before. But we must hurry so we will get to the Rainbow Paint Pool in time."

Maxi and Mini were glad to see the stable boy again. He showed them where they could find the paint buckets. There were tiny buckets and little paint buckets, middle-size paint buckets and super middle-size buckets. There were big buckets and giant buckets.

"Grab one, and let's go!" said Maxi.

As soon as Maxi and Mini had each put a bucket into the pony cart they headed toward Rainbow Paint Pool. The Pippins were anxiously waiting for them.

"Hurry!" said Peppermint Pippin. "We must be ready to paint the rainbow when it's time."

"Here are the brushes," said Lollipop Pippin.

"Fill up your buckets and follow us," said Gumdrop Pippin.

Maxi and Mini filled their buckets with rainbow paint and got ready to paint the rainbow. Then Gingerbread Pippin saw their buckets.

"Oh, no!" he said. "Look at those buckets!"

Everyone looked at Mini's bucket. It was SO tiny.

"Why didn't you bring a bigger bucket?" asked Peppermint Pippin. "You can't paint much of a rainbow with that."

"I...I thought that the paint was too valuable," said Mini. "So I thought I should get only a little of it."

Then everyone looked at Maxi's bucket. It was middle-size. "Why didn't you bring a bigger bucket?" asked Peppermint Pippin. "You can't paint much of a rainbow with that."

"I guess I thought what Mini thought," said Maxi. "Perhaps I thought a little bigger, but not much."

Then Maxi and Mini saw the bucket the pippins had brought. It wasn't really a bucket at all, but a giant pot. And it was filled with rainbow paint.

"It's time to paint!" Peppermint Pippin shouted. "Let's go!"

Mini started. But she was soon out of paint. Her rainbow was no higher than a stump.

Maxi was next. But he was soon out of paint. His rainbow was no higher than the pony cart.

The pippins went to work with their pot of rainbow paint. They painted the most beautiful rainbow you have ever seen.

"I...I guess I learned something special," said Mini. "My rainbow will be no bigger than the size of my paint bucket."

"Poppi said one time that Jesus gives us no more than our prayer bucket will hold," said Maxi. "Believe He'll do a little, He will do it. Believe He'll do a lot, and He will do that, too."

LET'S TALK ABOUT THIS

What this story teaches: Your rainbow will be no bigger than the size of your paint bucket. Jesus will give you only as much as your "prayer bucket" will hold.

1. How could Maxi and Mini have painted a bigger rainbow?

2. What did the size of their bucket have to do with the size of their rainbow?

3. What did Maxi mean by the size of your "prayer bucket"?

4. Jesus will give you only what you truly believe He will give. Remember the Bible story about Bartimaeus? How was this true of him?

Zacchaeus—
Greedy Man of Jericho
Luke 19:1-10

Zacchaeus was a rich little man. He had a good job and made lots of money. He lived in a beautiful home. But Zacchaeus had almost no friends.

That's because Zacchaeus was a tax collector. Nobody liked tax collectors. They made people pay money to the Romans, the foreigners who ruled their land. They made people pay more than they should. And they stole part of the money for themselves.

Zacchaeus was a greedy man. He made himself rich by making other people poor. How could such a man have many friends?

Zacchaeus was lonely. He wanted friends. He wanted a good friend. But who would be his friend?

Then Zacchaeus heard that Jesus was in Jericho. He heard that Jesus was coming down the road where he was standing.

Zacchaeus waited. Then he saw a big crowd moving down the road. Jesus was in the middle of the crowd. How could he ever see Jesus among so many people? Zacchaeus was a short man. He could not hope to see over those other people.

Then Zacchaeus had an idea. He ran down the road and climbed into a sycamore tree. He sat on a big branch hanging over the road. Jesus would come under that branch, and he would certainly see Him then.

Zacchaeus was excited as he watched the crowd come closer and closer. Then he saw Jesus!

Jesus also saw Zacchaeus. He stopped and looked up at Zacchaeus, sitting in the big tree. Zacchaeus was surprised. Jesus was looking at him!

"Zacchaeus, come down from there!" Jesus said. "I want to stay at your house today."

Now Zacchaeus was even more surprised. Jesus wanted to come to his house? Jesus wanted to be his good friend? Zacchaeus was so happy!

But some of the neighbors were not happy. "Jesus is going to the house of a very bad man!" they complained.

Zacchaeus did not want to be a bad man anymore. He told Jesus, his neighbors, and even the strangers that he wanted to turn away from his sins. He wanted to follow Jesus.

"If I have cheated anyone, I will pay him back four times as much," Zacchaeus said. "I also will give half of all I own for the poor."

Jesus was pleased with Zacchaeus. He knew that Zacchaeus would not be greedy now. He knew that Zacchaeus would turn from his sin and follow Jesus.

"Salvation has come to this house today!" Jesus said. Even greedy little Zacchaeus, the hated tax collector, could be saved from his sin! Even this bad little man could accept Jesus and follow Him!

Then Jesus told the people why He had come to earth. "I came to seek and to save people who are lost." Jesus came to change each one of us so we may live forever with Him in heaven.

WHAT DO YOU THINK?
What this story teaches: People who live bad lives cannot expect to have good friends. But Jesus wants to change each of us so that we can live with Him forever.
1. What kind of person was Zacchaeus before he met Jesus? What did he do that was bad?
2. How did he change when he met Jesus? What does Jesus want to do for each one of us?

Pippin Treasure

A Muffin Make-believe Story

"Time to go home!" said Captain Maxi.

"It's been so much fun on this special island," Mini added. "But Captain Maxi is right. It is time to go home."

The four pippins looked sad. "People don't often visit us here," they said. "You are such fun people. Ruff and Tuff are fun, too."

The pippins looked even more sad as Captain Maxi and his crew took the painted ponies and pony cart back to Painted Pony Stables. Maxi, Mini, Ruff, and Tuff looked sad, too, as they said good-bye to the stable boy.

"Time to board the Golden Tub!" Captain Maxi ordered.

"Aye, aye, Captain!" said Mini.

Ruff barked, Tuff meowed, and the crew headed toward the beach with the pippins. But halfway there the pippins stopped and whispered to one another.

"We have a gift for you to take with you," Peppermint Pippin said happily. "We'll stop at Pippin's Place to pick it up."

You can imagine how surprised Maxi and Mini were when they saw the gift. Peppermint Pippin opened a treasure chest filled with beautiful peppermint sticks. Gumdrop Pippin opened a treasure chest filled with beautiful gumdrops. Gingerbread Pippin opened a treasure chest filled with beautiful gingerbread men. And Lollipop Pippin opened a treasure chest filled with beautiful lollipops.

Maxi's eyes sparkled. So did Mini's eyes. They had never seen such wonderful treasure.

"We never give our treasures to anyone," said Peppermint Pippin. "But we want to give you a special gift."

"Oh, thank you, thank you," said Mini. She carefully took one of each.

But Maxi was so dazzled that he even forgot to say thank you. Instead he went from one chest to another, greedily stuffing his pockets. Mini was so ashamed. The pippins were ashamed of Maxi, too, but they didn't know what to do.

"Captain Maxi!" Mini shouted. But Maxi kept on stuffing his pockets.

Then Mini stood in front of the gumdrop chest, where Maxi was headed next. She folded her arms and stared at Maxi.

"Maxi Muffin! What does Jesus think of you now?" she said.

Maxi stopped where he was. Suddenly he remembered the picture of Jesus on his wall. He could see Jesus looking at him.

Greedy Maxi gulped. What DID Jesus think of him now? Maxi was ashamed. One by one, he put the lollipops, gumdrops, peppermint sticks, and gingerbread men back into the chests.

"Please keep one of each," said Peppermint Pippin.

"I...I'm so sorry I let Greedy Maxi take over," Maxi told Mini and the pippins. "Jesus isn't pleased when that happens."

"I'm glad you remembered that you belong to Jesus, Maxi," said Mini.

"So am I!" said Maxi.

Then Captain Maxi and his friends boarded the Golden Tub, hoisted the sail and let the winds of imagination take them back to Maxi's and Mini's backyard.

LET'S TALK ABOUT THIS

What this story teaches: Jesus changes us and helps us do things that please Him.

1. Do you remember the Bible story about Zacchaeus? How did Jesus change Zacchaeus?

2. Have you ever accepted Jesus as your Savior? When you do, He will change your life so you will want to please Him and live for Him. Would you like Him to do that now? Ask Him! He will.

3. Perhaps you already have accepted Jesus, but like Maxi, you have a problem and want Jesus to help you. Ask Him! He wants you to please Him in all things.

Mini's Word List

Twelve words that all Minis and Maxis want to know:

BLIND–Blind people in Bible times had many troubles. Few people wanted to hire them, so they had to beg for a living. This meant that blind people were often very poor. Without good medicines at that time, many people were blind.

BOOTH–Workers in the hot fields often made little houses of limbs and leaves. Booths were also used like tents when people came to some feasts in Jerusalem.

CLOAK–Sometimes the Bible calls a cloak a coat. The cloak was like a light robe, worn loosely over the shoulders.

DEBT, DEBTOR–People in Bible times were either rich or poor. When poor people owed money and could not pay their debt, they were often thrown into prison. Sometimes wives or children were sold as slaves to help pay this debt.

DREAM–The Bible tells of many dreams. Some had special meaning. Often God spoke to people through their dreams.

FOREVER–The Bible tells us that we will keep on living with Jesus in heaven if we accepted Him as our Savior here on earth. Our bodies die, but we never die.

GOD'S HOUSE–Your church is God's house, a place where you go to worship Him. In Bible times the Tabernacle, or the Temple, was God's house.

HELL–Hell is a place where people are punished when they leave this earth. Heaven is a place where people live with Jesus happily when they leave this earth. We live with Jesus if we accept Him as our Savior.

MESSENGER–People who took news from one to another were messengers. The news may have been good or bad.

NEEDLE'S EYE–Bible-time needles looked much like ours today. Thread was pushed through the "eye" of the needle. Some say the small gate within a big city gate was also called a needle's eye.

SERVANT–A slave worked for people but was not paid for the work. A servant was paid. Some slaves did the same work that servants did.

TAXES–As long ago as Bible times, governments have made people pay money to help them do their work. This money is called taxes. In Jesus' time the Temple also had taxes. Each person had to pay a small amount each year to support the work at the Temple.

Moody Press, a ministry of the Moody Bible Institute is designed for education, evangelization, and edification. If we may assist you in knowing more about Christ and the Christian Life, please write us without obligation: Moody Press, c/o MLM, Chicago, Illinois 60610.